dead
man's
float

For MIKE,
ONE OF THE FEW
GOOD READERS,
WITH BEST WISHES
ALSO FROM THE "COVER GIRL,"

Other Works by Derk Wynand

Poetry

Locus, 1971

Snowscapes, 1974

Pointwise, 1979

Second Person, 1983

Fetishistic, 1984

Heat Waves, 1988

Airborne, 1994

Door Slowly Closing, 1995

Closer to Home, 1997

Fiction

One Cook, Once Dreaming, 1980

Translations

*Under the Cover of a Hat /
Green-sealed Message*, 1985
(from the German of H.C. Artmann)

Sweat and Industry, 1992
(from the German of H.C. Artmann)

The Quest for Dr U., with Malcolm Green, 1993
(from the German of H.C. Artmann)

Black Sails, 1999
(from the Serman of Erich Wolfgang Skwara)

dead man's float

Derk Wynand

Brick Books

National Library of Canada Cataloguing in Publication Data

Wynand, Derk, 1944–
    Dead man's float

Poems.
ISBN 1-894078-20-9

    1. Title

PS8595.Y58D42 2002   C811'.54   C2001-904094-6
PR9199.3.W9D42 2002

We acknowledge the support of the Canada Council for the Arts
for our publishing programme. The support of the Ontario Arts
Council is also gratefully acknowledged. We acknowledge the
financial support of the Government of Canada through the Book
Publishing Industry Development Program (BPIDP) for our
publishing activities.

The cover art is Eva Wynand's, "Dead Man's Float," acrylic on
canvas, 36 in. x 48 in., 2000.
The author's photograph was taken by Eva Wynand.

This book is set in Minion, Sabon and Trixie.

Design and layout by Alan Siu.

Printed and bound by Sunville Printco Inc.

Brick Books
431 Boler Road, Box 20081
London, Ontario   N6K 4G6

brick.books@sympatico.ca

For Eva, who led me toward many of these poems, and for our mothers, who led too, but did not see us reach them all.

Contents

III. Night Window

I. Creature Comforts

Heron

Into a quiet just like this
more than the proverbial pin
might drop,

or distant swell break
in which you keep finding yourself,
swimming.

Nearer the shore, a heron
you no longer see stabs
and stabs at invisible fish.

How dangerous a weapon,
the head.

Pigeons

High in the tula tree's branches
where the real power lies, above
rich and poor, whatever sets them apart,
the pigeons gather and come
undone. They drop one by one to
the ground where the crumbs lie scattered,
down to the cobblestones, pecking,
picking out the good from the bad.
Then drift beneath the tables for
grasshoppers, peanuts, beer, for spills
and shells, and give the winers and
diners hungry, almost holy
looks before casting off the weight
that keeps them earthbound. And so they
rise again in pairs to the crown
of the tree where the noise must go
small: distant human mutterings
that up there must sound and resound
like petitions or like prayers.

Parrot

A parrot bows on top of its cage, paces
and bows, as if still inside, down to the bits
of melon and corn. Looking at you sideways,
it gives nothing away, like any worker
in the tourist industry. Having robbed it
already of its pride, do you want its corn
too? Wait a minute, what is it giving you
the little eyeball for? You have had nothing
to do with building the cage or placing it
to attract a few customers for who knows
what business here on the sidewalk among
the hibiscus bushes and VW
beetles that stink up the air. The cage door stays
open all day: the parrot can come and go
as it likes, can it not? Into the bowl placed
to one side you are more than welcome to toss
coins or fruit, maybe a thumb – and learn besides
its small language: *gracias gringo go home.*

Pelican

I.

Beak into your chest like a petulant child
or passive monk, then opening it slowly
to see whether or what the world
has provided – no leper's thumb here,
though the ocean could no doubt heave up
something equally disgusting to test
your faith, jellyfish with its poisons,
or sea serpent. Would you eat them
without hesitation as a different legend
demands? Or hold them in the vastness
of your bill until your faith returned?
The waves rocking you rock you
without changing the least thing
in the face you turn to the world.

II.

Icon of patience, whether up
in the air or bobbing down
on the swell: we learn from you
even if you make no claims
to be a teacher. What's to learn?

The air supports the unlikely balance
of your beak, belly and wings,
and when the surface of the water
flashes with frantic perch or bream,
you fold up and drop to claim your reward.

Then, beak and belly full, you cork
once more on calmer water,
with a childlike or a monkish grin.

Mid-life Crisis

A robin appears to have fallen out
of love with his image in the window,
stupid and more stupid against the glass,
beating his brains out, what little he has,
with every blow scrawnier. No idea
what he thinks he's protecting, what love nest
he may have built in the alders nearby.
Here, one robin looks much like another,
a bird with orange feathers and much drab:
a creature that likes worms and makes a fuss
over them. Stupid against the window
for days, he is finally slowing down
just a little, his brain numbed, or heavy
with the suspicion that whatever stirs
in the glass may be neither robin nor
male. Time and again he eyes his own image
aslant, as if feigning lack of interest,
a huge abstraction keeping him busy.

Hound

in the distance, yowling away, no one
and nothing answering.

No visible moon he could be howling at,
and the bitches not in heat, not clinging
for a change or overly affectionate.

What can the neighbours be up to
in their waking, or their sheets?

A prolonged note or vibration strums
repeatedly up a tighter and tighter nerve,
shifts into more anxious mode:

Careful, my man's best friend,
my little monotonous songster.

Mexican Dogs

Perros: already the poets
have made much of you,
not that you're much to behold,
nor that you do much
to stir us to love you or fear.
For the most part, you seem
content to lie in the shade
of walls or cars, and hardly
care if the walls threaten
to come tumbling down
or the cars start up. Passive
in the heat of day and amorous
presumably by night, you leave
the dugs of the *perras* swollen.
Or are you depressive day
and night? Near-suicidal?
When men pass by,
you look up sadly, checking
for the hidden rock.
When women approach
with empty hands,
you look sad also,
but less alone.

Regional Museum

I. DOGS

Or is it coyotes, is it foxes,
all terracotta blown
like balloons or like glass?

II. TORTOISE

with its human eyes
and its human limbs
and its shell.

III. DESNUDO

Ambiguous figure, male
or female – oops.
It's female.

IV. SERPENT

Terracotta wound
around the bowl, around
into memory, perfect container
perfectly contained.

Hermit Crab

If *you* think of yourself as a hermit
I understand – the world's not much
to sing or think about, but without
a navel, what do you contemplate
when you sink into your hole?

Back from their long night fishing,
the fishermen are cutting up sharks,
and washing the cleaned fish
in what seems polluted water.
Will the surviving sharks answer
the call of such mixed blood?

Nothing much here evokes the purity
hermits must constantly be seeking,
unless it is the dark of your hole in sand
you escape to, or the charged quiet
on the ocean bottom far from shore.

Gecko

I.

a glimpse

gecko behind the mirror
where your head is
vanishing

quick as a thought
an afterthought

it seemed to turn
once maybe
also thinking of you

before it lost its own thread

outside the surf breaks
and breaks as if
marking time

no moon or man
reflects on it

II.

How could anyone
not adore you,
little devourer of
large moths, sticky
ceiling-hanger, light-
lurker, master of
stillness whenever it
suits you? And
if not "adore,"
then "like," friend
at least, enemy
of the enemy
mosquito? Your traces
on the white
walls put some
women off, those
who must clean
them. Not men
who dream of
hunting, of the
quick kill, and
lift not one
finger, keeping almost
as perfectly still
as you do,
until the women
come after you
with their mops
and their brooms.

III.

Earth-coloured, verging
on the albino, upside-down
on the ceiling or clinging
to the wall by the light
that draws mosquitoes
and moths. One inches –
no, *millimetres* up
to a wasp almost as large
as it is, gives it the eye
slowly and long, gives it
both its black eyes, then
thinks better of it:
a week's supply of food
gone up in the smoke
of the wasp's barbed tail.
The gecko retreats
toward one of its mates,
nips at its head, bumps.
Gecko foreplay or mere
territorial posturing? What
to us seems infinite,
the supply of mosquitoes
and moths, in the eyes
of the gecko must seem
limited. Far out at sea,
the fishermen must
understand gecko thinking:
they never stop fishing
for more than their share.
Gecko stomach, human
stomach – how think at all
when these need feeding?

IV.

A chirping or clicking at night, long past
the time for birds, and no bats behind
the mirror or picture frame from which it issues.
A chirping outside – in answer? Answering
what question, what gecko-need to know
that others are around? A mating or
a wake-up call? We'll never know. Tonight,
the villagers pay tribute to Our Lady
of Guadeloupe. They're cranking up
the music, firing their rifles, aiming rockets
into the dark. They're drinking mescal
down to the worm. Even the roosters
are in high fiesta mode, crowing hours
before the sunrise, agitating so that others
in the flock squawk along. Our Lady
gets the full Pancho Villa treatment, Emiliano
Zapata, Benito Juárez. Even the steady ocean
wobbles, the surf breaking harder on the ear,
on the rocks below. All night, the night looms
loud and large, providing only small silences
for a gecko maybe feeling small, and lacking
the comforts of religion or politics or family.

An Iguana

climbs slow-motion through the liana up
the palm tree, tail a mock air root, lime-green,
breathing the heat in slowly for hours.
Later, in less, more beautiful light, though
time here and light seem to matter no more
nor less than they do elsewhere, two tourists
of indeterminate sex push and are
pushed through chest-high water in a semblance
of love the water's surface complicates.
Someone behind a palm tree is watching.
Could it be me, behind the half-parted
curtains, thinking it you? Humidity
and heat have split the air itself into
impossible atoms that recombine
into something only a little more
likely: a shadow, a fleeting thought, caught
and held just enough to make, first the eye,
then the mind unsure again. Particles
of light add up to a shifting contour,
waves of green on the green of liana
or rumpled sheet on which a body stirs
or appears to stir. Then disappears,
nothing again in the complex shadows
of the lianas or palm tree or bed
where the iguana was, shifting higher
or deeper, back into where this began.

Frog

As if you were witness, eyes
all on us, and ears (hidden)
on us too.

My lamentations, your lamentations.
Witness to what?

The mosquitoes go on today
as if nothing had happened,
leaving their infuriating mark
that marks nothing.

The nothing that's happened to us.

Frog, why don't you eat them? Stick
your tongue out, say something,
eat them.

Just don't turn your back
on us now that the mosquitoes
have made our dreams start to burn
closer and closer to the surface of sleep,
and the itch radiate out from the brain
and lower.

So low that when we wake,
we blush for real shame.

Witness to all of it, frog,
why don't you say something?
Come out of hiding and make
this awful silence pass.

Crickets

Solid as the idea
of bells, of the breath,
once they fall silent.

Blaming the Crane Flies

Cold front: one grey sneaks into another,
light assuming familiar sad tones,
first over the horizon, then closer.

Inside, she clings to a bluer sky and water
as the shadow grows up her arms
and puts on body there, weight.

In time, she gives in to the mood:
winter must be on its way.

Crane flies, as if resigned too, stop bouncing
along the ceiling and hang there, caught up
in the play of light and dark
over the shadowy folds of the curtains.

In a nearly colourless grass outside,
she'll later find tiny brown pouches,
insect slough, the "leather" of these leatherjackets
passing on their lives again.

Spider

The one who pays me visits every five minutes
or so, without checking ahead (having no phone
or to me comprehensible communication system),
also upsets whatever osmotic or gravitational force
that makes the condensation adhere to the beer can
beside my journal, until only seconds ago dry and
spiderless. I don't know if he or she is spider enough
to spin webs like its prototype, to go away and pick
on someone more his own size, or if his bite is
(will be) worse than that of the mosquitoes we dread
for the dreams they deliver, dengue fever, malarial
hallucinations. His poison, at least, is almost
entirely of his own making, leaving a small doubt
about and a little faith in the lord and mistress
of creation, while the two of us sit here, or perch
proverbially spring-like, and spin our thoughts out,
or what for spiders must pass for thoughts,
out along the invisible line that time is, passing.

Dragonflies

Two of them
mating, a pair

suspended in air
heavier than what

their frantic wings
seem made of.

When the sun
reflects off them

at just the
right angle (it

depends on where
and who you

think you are)
their wings and

their bodies, perfectly,
begin to disappear.

Tropical Moth

Large as a small bat
and inside the house as fleshy
when you slap at it in vain,

ominous in its black feathers
as any bird that's found an entry,
and attractive as any death wish –

yes, it draws the eye,
the hand, the full burden
of the mind –

and when opened screens
and windows allow an escape,
your heart goes fluttering after it.

Wasp Nest

I. MEXICAN TIME

Modest beneath the thatched roof,
small wonder, just a handful
of wasps clinging to it in the heat
and the wind, the work
progressing slowly, slowly,
or not at all.

II. CONDITION OF THE WORKERS

Such a humble structure beneath the fronds
of the palapa, just room enough
for the larvae, and not many of those
inside their papery cells,
while the adults sleep outside
where the air is better.

Wasps

I.

Poison in a finger appears to work under the skin, flesh pressing harder behind the nail. Soft now, soft, it tightens with the surfeit of blood, white cell and red stirred by the memory of a wasp curled on skin, clinging there despite the hand swatting at it days later.

II.

Not far enough in the distance, someone plays Mozart too loud, the motifs broken by firs and oaks and here and there the Nylons or Stones, stuff of a later music we don't like much. Even Mozart, answering mostly to a neighbour's needs, leaves us untouched.

Foiled time and again by its screen, the wasps stick to our window and do not give up. Guessing a purpose behind their explorations of an empty plane, we can almost tolerate their menacing buzz.

III.

No ideas, still, though plenty of things, papery nest abandoned in the arbutus, clack of leaf against leaf as October approaches. What wasps remain have gone stupid, in front of our faces holding to no identifiable pattern or hovering too close to what space cuff of shirt or jeans allows. We refuse to give up our positions on the sun deck, even now that the sun has lost its heat. Short sentences grow slowly out of the individual words we summon from wasp, arbutus, sun, and only much later: the paragraphs of their absence.

Mosquito

I.

Just one, distracting from
what must be others,
not here,
never there,
in the tropics
worrisome.

II.

The cathedral of Sto. Domingo
large outside and inside
a statue of Sto. Domingo, smaller,
and a solitary cactus there,
here the gallery walls,
cactus and art and everything
stinging.

III.

Virtual only, platonic buzz
and silence and bite,
sneaking without Socratic method
into the way we imagine reality.

IV.

Segue by way of Plato:

the sun serves as idea
and icon of the real
and into it, Dracula,
you seem to disappear.

V.

The butterfly also has a proboscis.
And the elephant.
And the rain god, Chac.

VI.

Larger now, squashed,
to airy thinness beat,
the blood too red exposed,
prompting dreams of malaria,
dengue – ridiculous,
your puffed-up sense of scale!

VII.

As a child I was told to grin
and bear the bite,
to give the anticoagulant poison
time to return to its host.
                    Quatsch!
Squashed then in German,
nonsense, in English
squashed again.

VIII.

Only the host (not heavenly)
for all that we fear, why should you
shoulder (or wing) all the blame,
bubonic insect, little flying black
death?

IX.

The business of your buzz,
the sting of your stingy nature,
your give and take and mostly
take, you bloodsucker.

X.

A Pacheco poem, illustrated
by Francisco Toledo (holy!
No storm) – mosquito as vampire,
exactly as I have it in **iv**, more
or less, great minds and
well maybe,
thinking, not thinking alike.

XI.

Silent conspiracy below the knees,
around the ankles, near the toes,
and no one with a sound theory
about it – let them develop theories
now that the blood's drawn
and the perpetrator gone.

XII.

What little you bring, we keep
for a day, a week, and slough off,
not like a skin, like a bad memory.

If you bring more, we suffer it
longer, so we're told after.
Memory in this case
does not serve.

XIII.

No friend of the gecko that hides
behind the mirror or by the lamp
to blindside you within its light.

No friend of the bat that knows
by heart or ear how to make sense
of your mazes of darkness.

"The enemy of my enemy..."?

Where are you in the mythologies
of those who have had to contend
with you, or benefit from your work?

Conquistador? Aztec?

xtabentun

a yellow song
of anise and honey

honey and anise
a bottle of *xtabentun*

honey the maya used
in their mortar so

says jimmy the mayan
guide at chichén itzà

informed by *xtabentun*
we slur out other uses

honey *miel* mead
european connections

quetzalcoatl another maybe
viking white god hmmm

hmmm humming
the mayas harder abuzz

II. Tropical Snowman

Correspondence

I.

The letters also appear to shake with the heat of age, of rage at whatever seems (seems only), what conspires to have them knock into one another like old and young men on a sidewalk wide enough to allow for safer passage, young women of course present too, they alone aware of the role they play at the peripheries of this metaphor, and the letters then fusing, confusing, though the women, *dear* readers all, have no trouble, their eyes blue and sharp, keeping them apart.

II.

... and the two of us are still on letters, getting them, writing, still *in* them somehow, the parts we mention stuffed into envelopes or lazing between lines the letters make, thinking, before we set pen to paper, how we still manage to stir responses from each other, both having long stopped believing in metaphor, sure the letters spell exactly what they want, so well have we pinned them down, or they us, though wanting, wanting the white – may I speak for you? – to be more than mere sheet or envelope, to be light, be truth, be all womankind, and this black more than just ink, though as dark, as true, as... male? We want, in short, the two, whatever we can make of them or they of themselves – if I may speak for myself – to reach out, wherever we are, want them only given and their meaning taken.

Impossibilities of Flight

The need to make or keep it simple, to answer and find answers.

To talk of birds into and out of trees and not miss all that flicker
and towhee evoke as they bicker for position around a
pond beneath the oaks.

Birds prove simple enough, Patrick's "flying things" simpler still,
unless these begin to evoke angels, ghosts and ghostly
divers jack-knifing through memory, Borges'
imaginary beings, snatches of music or thought,
relentless horizon note or recurrent dream
of a flight just before it breaks into
hopeless complexity.

Whose needs do such fragments address in September 1994?

Whose after?

Remembered flesh keeps recomposing itself in a mind that propels
it in its own directions: the body can hardly resist.

Skin contains it, the lip soft when words pass over or conjure it,
the tongue giving rise to the idea of softness or just being
soft, on the lip first and then not Platonic at all
– *yes, yes*:

first and last word you have been flying from and toward, air
sucked in and burned and released as the all too human
engines have done.

Tropical Snowman
for Eva

A love poem, this, note and admission to you
who painted it, one of its subjects, him (me?)
snowy, bent over not quite backwards in parody
perhaps of what critics might call "desire."
For you, no doubt for me, the sunflower only
shines down on him, sun balloon at the end
of the little string he clings to. Too thin.
He offers it to her, (I to you), sun or balloon
or aching token of the heart, arcing high
over the other curves you've layered artfully
one over the other, the seeming accidents rendered
deliberate now, brushwork that does not have her
brushing him off (you, me). So I need to think.
This note, like your painting, wants to be
its own illustration, the words, no less
than the paint, a likely cover-up. Can there be
an accurate medium for this? And because
I have read your reading me into your work,
I sketch us into mine also, hopeful, the carrot
of my nose pointing ever toward you,
without compass finding the right direction,
as I think you'd have it. I agree. And
you've given us real arms and legs, not sticks!
Yes, of course it's self-referential – or is it
reflexive? – the cozy vacuum of our lives
promising to keep us warm as coffee or soup,
and me, presumably snow or ice before, now melting
toward you, and you, without pretence to modesty,
claiming those classic lines you have given yourself.
And while you don't return my gaze, neither do you
refuse it. No, this work catches us well enough,
you with your dreams of steamier climates,
me with mine of chasing after you south.

Dream of the State of the World

Fragments again: a paddle, a wheel or wheels
in the air or water, a ship taking someone
to some destination – Vancouver, Gorazde,
Sarajevo, God help him. A vessel on a mission
of mercy. The plane releases its foils and flares
and comes down too hard. Help has finally arrived.
At the Olympics, now as then, the athletes shed
their sweatshirts and nationalities;
they have nothing left to trade, having given
their all already, as the sportscasters say,
the nationalists. But the flags still fly,
as do the snipers' bullets and relief planes.
Deep inside their language, a few poets still manage
to stutter, singers to sing at least for themselves,
not knowing what else they can do. One poet leads:
prose victorious. Video more so: snipers fire, yes,
the bitter poets, not very effective. They've run
out of ammunition and keep on shooting – strategy,
that old joke, good enough to repeat when everything
and everyone repeat themselves: propagandists,
publishers, politicians, all the members
of the Security Councils who talk in slow circles,
mercy and mercy and mercy asked for, not given.

Golden Age, Maybe Sepia

The folks in which other folks
might take an interest, or show –
eyes wider, suddenly, head turned
without violence to accommodate
every sidelong glance. In the photo,
at least, they always seem to put on
a pretty good act, convincing – whom?

They come into the corner store, gather
around the wood stove everyone still
half-remembers. It's winter, of course –
heart and body need nothing so much
as warmth. Yes, the age is forever wanting
to be golden, plain folks not content just
to sit around a stove when they could be
dancing in a circle around more ancient fire,
circle and fire and a song composed
to fit in – these the adequate magic
that allows "plain folks" to rise out
of themselves and slip into better roles.

And look at them now, talking their heads off,
while we only look at the photos and strain
to hear, nodding light-headed, all light, all dark,
and all that comes between.

Knot

Hard to believe, here where cherry trees spring into
softest pinks as in water-colours awash with

an untroubling Zen – here and now, lover cuffs
lover, or ties the lightest silk around ankle

and wrist, and maybe a gag in the mouth to stop
little outbursts of . . . what? . . . joy?... fear?... from breaking

the mood of the scene. What an exquisite tension!
But you only daydream all this. It's cruel April:

even an older man's thoughts must turn to something.
Maybe it's silk that restrains you, that holds more than

just the voice down, keeping it down, soft. What a time
for jokes! Beyond the serious orchard in which

you have long made a habit of seeking comfort
in the caterpillars wound into their cocoons

or spinning on threads – yes, silken – you imagine
a far thicker, harder rope that burns, tightens, cuts.

Voyage

It begins and ends on a blue note:
a Steller's jay knocked cold against the glass,
and cold more slowly on the ground
after long gasping for balance and air
and spitting of not much blood. On the news,
too many scraps of metal and flesh refuse
to fit into the idea of a plane, the earth
scorched in a close circle around. Inside it,
a ludicrous burned shoe, charred ballpoint
or comb. Yes, the earth itself appears to go
up in smoke. Can the jay, we wonder, still feel
anything. Should we carry it somewhere
out of reach of the neighbourhood cats?
Can any suffering be anything but long?
Our silence does not lead us to any larger thought.
Though we do not say it, flight all at once
seems less miraculous, then more:
We know what can happen and fly.

Some People Going Somewhere

I. MUSTANG

The woman behind the wheel of her new Mustang refuses
to give up. She stays on the tail of the truck with its load
of lumber and tries to pass. Every time the road straightens,
another car approaches, or one more truck.

The driver in front gears down or gears up, in his mirror
watching the woman on his tail fall back, move in, fall back.
Now and then, she manoeuvres into his blind spot and stays there
a while before she reappears. He gives this deliberate thought:
his blind spot. And wonders, too, about certain women
who have all the time in the world.

Maintaining speed, he follows the road and does not pull
over or signal when it looks safe. If she's going to pass him,
she'll have to take her chances.

II. LINE

She stands in line and concentrates on the number
someone a long time ago pressed into her hand.
Ahead of her, a man goes grey before her eyes.
Behind her, a man coughs, then talks to himself
or anyone else who has no choice but to listen.
Once every half hour or hour, they all move forward one step.

She could cough or turn grey, but what good would it do?
The man in front of her goes white, finally ready to drop.
The man behind her coughs, having found no convincing answer
to the one question he's asked.

When the next hour strikes, maybe,
she will make her move.

III. RUSH HOUR

The traffic stalls, its gases still rushing into the air.
On some urgent business, a woman keeps pushing ahead.
The tobacconists have brought in their metal stands on which
newspapers once proclaimed the relative importance of things.
Her name has not appeared in the headlines; her photograph
has not graced the racks.

The motors idle louder; horns continue to blare.
Passengers try in vain to force open the windows of buses
making no progress. They wave at the woman leaving them
behind, as though to warn her of stories still in the making.

At her back, a man spits and settles his arms on the bench
that affords him the best view of whatever will happen and
not happen. Somewhere ahead – but who can say
what lies ahead? The man, at least, can relax; he knows
he's not going anywhere.

Without such certainties, the woman walks on,
through the snarled, snarling traffic, beneath locked windows
behind which human beings pray for her, and past
urgent messages drying slowly on the walls.

IV. SUNDAY DRIVERS

In their automatic – he at the wheel, she along for the ride –
they stare at the red light, the more promising idea of green
fixed lower, a tension in their calves.

He keeps one foot on the gas, one on the brake pedal
and, in her own way, she does the same.

For most of their lives, of their one life together,
they have been driving and not driving like this, seat belts on,
clandestine air bags folded away in front of them,
their feet on the real, the imagined pedals.

The insurance papers in the glove compartment double
into themselves and the registration.
Maps of the continent offer up their little risk:
once off the island, the ferry, they can just keep going
and going almost anywhere.

They have money – what's stopping them?

No traffic on the road tonight, no ghost cars or hidden cameras,
but only a red light that refuses to change, and the two of them
facing it together, brake gas brake gas,
ready to go or to stay.

Courtyard

Stones on top of the walls that defined the courtyard appeared softened in time by geraniums, their many pink mouths. Or the intense sunlight softened them, beating down on them until we could almost see them crumble. How foolish the intruder who might have tried to scale them, the mouths all shouting at once, every leaf and blossom raising the alarm, impossible to ignore. For all that undisturbed, we whiled away the late morning and afternoon hours, dozing, daydreaming, dreaming, the same or at least very similar garden hose watering both the real flowerbeds and those of our dreams.

Despite her black coat, the dog chose a sunlit spot to lie in. She closed her eyes, panted almost fiercely, to the point of suffering – ours, at least – and did not seek shade. From time to time, she whimpered, her legs twitching, a sure sign she was dreaming also.

On the greenest leaves, aphids let black ants milk them. Too fascinated or squeamish to crush them between our fingers, and reluctant to spray the recently transplanted shrubs, we squinted down at them, forcing our eyes to focus. It seemed that important questions here demanded answers, but in this heat we could not come up with any.

From time to time, someone would rise, wipe sleeve or handkerchief across a wet brow, and pace back and forth on the white gravel, against the patterns raked into it by the gardener: parallel lines, concentric circles, waves. The sound of the disturbed gravel startled us at first, as did the sight of its broken lines, but slowly our eyes and ears came to terms with that. We accepted it, as we did everything else. No one picked up the rake to restore the order. The dog raised her head once, only bothering to open one eye, and relaxed again. We nodded off too.

The high wooden gate, its dark green a good background for the geraniums' pink, opened then, offering a glimpse of the city. Cars drove by, honking, though not, apparently, at us. Pedestrians, dressed in importantly dark suits and carrying important briefcases or purses, hurried along without turning their heads. When the geraniums complained, almost audibly, the startled visitor muttered something – a slurred apology maybe: the brandy, the heat, his head, his stomach – then closed the gate behind him, to our great relief restoring the silence and the balance.

Portuguese Market

How simply it proceeds:
                    the rich
can afford to throw coins
and the poor cannot afford
to reject them.
                    At the market,
the same money buys the same goods.

Refugees from Guinea-Bissau
try not to bite their lips on the streets
of Lisbon and Cascais,
                    buckets
of sardines and squid up for sale.

One slides a hand into her blouse –
this infernal heat –
                    and another wonders
what else she might sell.

But it's *his* image,
                    not hers
and so their reality finds itself
betrayed again.

He does not want her fish,
nor does she,
                    though
they do not want it differently.

He cannot pay her otherwise,
or toss her a coin –
                    beggar.

In the bucket,
the bluest eyes
of squid stare out at him
from the palest,
                    pink flesh.

Monument of the Discoveries

Come to a standstill at last, he watches
the familiar moon of his nail rise
into the strange blackness of blood.

Copper's been found and shipped home, silver,
gold. *Home* – the concept detaches itself from,
reattaches itself to the known.

A slave he thinks his lover tenses her belly,
renders all his thoughts less urgent for now,
flesh calling him back to a surer thing.

What a narrow gate opens to heaven,
and hell to pay when his wife finds out,
she, too, mere idea each night cast adrift.

Every day he wakes to a blacker bread
that breaks in his hands, its hard crumbs
a constellation that does not guide him.

Planets and moons rise and set into the green
where lemons spin, mandarins. A wet nurse
charts the stars in the eyes of his bastards.

Now compass and sextant have tarnished,
more practical lines and nets are beginning
to tangle. All the loved ones say *Yes!*

And *No!* In the space between, just time enough
to catch his breath, by the edge of the fire
where he sees shadow upon shadow flickering.

Lisbon

Mexican Walk

I.

At three, it all slows down,
the body crawling into
its own shadow, the shadow hot
on the heels of those
who can afford shoes
and of the barefoot also.

Step, stop, step and so
everything goes, slowly
down in the sun into shade,
beneath the tula tree now
and then pausing.

II.

Husband and wife, out on Sunday
the first time in months, on show
side by side, bellies foremost,
no tourist daring to raise his camera
to capture the photo finish.

A missed opportunity, this double
pregnancy: for him, no real labour,
and for her, not the least sign
on her face to suggest a moment
of real pleasure she cares to remember.

III.

Beneath the tulas in the zocalo,
the mothers who do not want
their photographs taken, their spirits
captured or destroyed, walk along
at adult speed and drag their kids
behind, breakneck. The leaves drop
from the tulas like nachos from the table,
and pigeons do not go after them.

IV.

Down at the hip, nearly below it,
some heat forcing the body forward,
while the head – the mind bent
on anything but walking –
drifts along not wholly parallel,
the whole person somehow making
visible progress,

not that it seems to matter so much
as that the hips swing, the head sways
along in that sunstroked way which lets
the mind give only its presence
and not its deepest content away.

These Tourists Think

they can go anywhere and they do, over
the broken glass lining the wall, through
the barbed wire over that and into
our private garden to sniff the hibiscus.
They nuzzle the bougainvillea and come up
empty-nosed, then head straight into
our bedroom just because
its wrought-iron door opens out onto
the patio and the screen's designed
to fend off only mosquitoes and wasps.
They walk in in a little group they think
offers them safety, keeping hands in pockets
or clutched to purses. Some whistle not at all
in harmony with the background jazz
we have put on the CD for anything but
this foreground, and compare us in our bed
to a photograph in their guidebook.
True, it bears a superficial resemblance, but
clearly it isn't us. No, we try to tell them, no,
our position here has nothing to do
with ignorant notions of Zapotec fertility.
No, the pillowslip's not for sale. They twist
their shirttails and noses into knots
and do not approve of our readings
of ourselves, the Zapotec, or Europeans.
Their guidebook has not failed them so far, so why
should it let them down now? They point
to the terracotta figures' unambiguous
arrangements, and to the smooth alabaster,
and nothing we do or say will convince them
that we're insignificant flesh and blood beneath
our one thin sheet, here in the cool bedroom
to which we've retreated only to escape
the relentless heat and noise of the sun.

Soledad Basilica

As light fades from day, the musicians
unsheathe their flutes, brass out their French horns
and tubas, tighten the strings of their fiddles,
fiddle with their guitars. Evening slowly releases
the last of its light, creates a new space
for dancing. A Zapotec woman twists pink
and blue strands of evening into the rug
she has been weaving, calls it a day.
The last light goes. The musicians stay,
letting the locals dance its memory back.

Behind the basilica, cripples perfecting
their own dance dance it until they find
the faith to toss braces and crutches aside,
walking sticks. Lame children begin to flex
their new precocity, swiping at adults
with useless cameras and coins clutched
and clutched in their mean fists.

The museum behind, nearly out of mind,
keeps making new room for darkness.
Into it crowd old news items, cartoons
and cartoonish drawings of Our Lady
of the Dead Donkey, burro miracle.
Chalices, crucifixes, trinkets, tokens,
relics here gather night and dust. Memory
piles up. The dust gathers darkness in
and begins to breathe. Tries to remember
dancing in light, in the gold that falls
through the window and across the dress
of pearls that adorns the Virgin who heals.

Turista Desnuda

Stupid or *macha* or merely thoughtless,
baking in the low sun without a care
in the world, unless it's for the pink
gloss of her breasts, each minute pinker,
more neon. None for flies, or shit,
or animal magnet for no real animals.
Most here ignore her as best as they can,
looking if at all as if by accident,
their looks glancing off, bouncing
off the water and quickly away
to the fishing boats nearby, bobbing
on the water or rolled up onto the beach
on logs, the pelicans bouncing also
on the surface, patient, sure something
will happen, fish or appreciative looks
and oohs and ahs from the tourists,
while the less patient frigate birds
strafe the gulls, startling their beaks
apart to release their catch and leave them
gaping, like the secret admirers
of the naked *turista*. But she lets nothing
drop from her jaws, no fish, no thanks
for the looks, no hook line sinker.
She's only here to bake in the sun,
to burn solo away from the men
and their boats and all the creatures
that float in the air or on water, rising
and sinking on it like her breasts
in whose honour they seem to do so.

Bad Music

Bad music insists, like bad musicians,
pushes itself to the front, stands
on its toes, cups its hands around
its mouth, elbows good silence aside –
so what? It's hungry. Its kids need
to be fed. Still, it's bad music. The strings
of its instruments keep coming unstrung,
the voice of the singer also. Its reeds go dry.
Bad music will be heard, like holy rollers
who push their Bibles through the eye
or mouth of a megaphone, camel message
that only slowly makes its way back down
to earth. Bad music only through tortuous
thinking can lead to heaven – the way
presence might suggest absence or
a beautiful girl the idea of death – but
it doesn't care. Its kids need to be fed
and it will be heard, no matter if no one
listens, if no one listens, very much.

Tourist

what is this what is this thank you
i'm learning the language what is this
thank you i'm trying where is the cathedral
thank you where is the currency exchange
the nearest museum thank you would you bring me
a glass of water please thank you two eggs
sunnyside up and a map of the city
thank you thank you how is your sister
your brother how many siblings comprise
your family is comprise the correct word
in this context thank you i'm trying does it show
thank you you're very kind what's showing
must be my effort or its fruits is fruits the right word
in this context thank you why thank you
where thank you do you find my jokes funny
what were your parents like did you have
a close bond with them is bond the right word
in this context why are you crying is it time
for me to go thank you have i overstayed
my welcome have i crossed any lines
why are you crying how much do i owe you
you're welcome

Language Skills

You will be pardoning me, but my wife
she speaks small Spanish and I speak
only one little, but more big. Most time
we know say fried eggs or eggs revolting
over breakfast and like fried potatoes.
My wife sometimes make errors and orders
fried Papa or – is not good – fried pope.
You will be understanding if as for me
I no understand the errors I do solo.
I have this time fifty-five anuses and
for because it is difficult learning Spanish.
The memory is not good. How many anuses
you have? Ah, so young! You speak
the English very well, more better than
my wife or mine, and your pronouncements
are very good also. They taste very good,
more better than we. What nationality
are we from? Ah, I understand:
you are thinking us gringos. But no,
señor, no – my wife she is Germany
and I Canada. Mexico is very good, it
tastes good and the peoples of Mexico also,
for because you are all the time fiesta
and much smile or is it laughter at us?

You Deal with the Spirits at Monte Alban

Once we *no-gracias* ourselves past the knick-knack peddlers
and offers for personalized tours in any of fifteen languages –

Español no problema, Deutsch bestimmt, Français qui sait?
and past the difficult ticket-taker irritated by our entry

by way of the exit, and once we take in the first full view
of the architectural and panoramic splendour, and fend off

the descendants of the natives who achieved it and who now
make masks as their ancestors did, of genuine resins derived

from the local trees and who knows what else, *barrato*,
almost as convincing as the partially reconstructed mask

at the Museo Rufino Tamayo far below, and once
we're finally alone at what purports to be the lodging

of a chieftain, a little maze of walls and stone without
the platform on which the athletes gave up their lives

if they won, no skulls chiselled all around, nor what priest
and conquistador thought dancers, you commune with whatever

spirits that touch you in the protective shade of the wall,
while I fuss and fluster over the hibiscus, the hummingbirds,

said to be ghosts of warriors slain in battle, the distant plain
that slowly seems to vanish into its own thickening haze.

Snorkelling at Pto. Angelito

Right now, it's the angel fish that appear to us,
a submarine host in golden variations,
hallelujah, and even if our mouths were not
clenched on our snorkels' mouthpieces, we would be
struck dumb by the play of watery light across
their bodies. Behind the coral, spotted eels seek
shelter, or snake away deeper behind the rocks
that throw shadows over their small mean heads. The look
on their small mean faces suggests that all is less
than perfect in this undersea garden. Something
bourgeois has entered it, like guilt about what is
merely thought. Like regret that follows no action.
The self-appointed lifeguard has warned us about
sea urchins that tend to break away from the rocks
and drift in closer to shore, where we slip out of
our fins. Too human again in our naked skins.
What brings such an abrupt milk to these clear waters?
No one can drink it. Schools of bream explode in front
of us, silver shrapnel tearing at our bodies
and minds. At our eyes. Our wounded hearts ache along
in their different directions. Could sharks have chased
the fish our way? Barracuda? Something forever
appears to be watching, below us. Over us.

Pulling in from the Rocks

Having fooled you, the tide keeps you drifting
toward the rocks with its barnacles, coral,
sea urchins, and me swimming minutes away
with my clumsy fins. In a controlled panic,
you call, just loud and hard enough to suggest
some urgency, not so much that I panic too.

Cramp? Sharks in the water? Jellyfish sting?
My amplified feet get me to you in time,
get us both slowly away from the rocks.

Relax. Put your mask in the water and float.
Let me do the work for a while, for once.

Something about this feels like a reversal.
Usually, I'm the one who is drifting, now closer,
now farther away, and never toward nor away
from anything so solid as rock.

You're the one who nudges me ahead or pulls me
back in. Relax. Relax for once and see: for all
your hard-earned doubts, it's still working.

III. Night Window

Cave

What are the eyes of others to you?
What are their ears?

Someone somewhere outside
carries a bad tune, badly, as if for herself alone,
a possibility that makes it no better.

You can hardly choose to listen or not listen.

So long as she's singing, how can she guess
what silence you want?

Though the stars by day appear
to shine just for you, the spaces between seem
to accommodate everyone.

Beneath them, the woman, if it is a woman,
sings a song that almost describes your condition.

In your cave, of which she seems to be singing,
something like the tail of a scorpion strikes
something like a head, until the idea of poison
begins to effect the idea of a cure.

Late October: What Started This

A contraction of the metals
or alloys in the thermostat
allowed for contact and made
the circuit close or is
it open and the heat
kicked in, the element grew
hotter, the little fan blew
over it until the room
warmed enough for the metals
or the alloys to expand
once more, breaking the circuit
so that the fan stopped
and the element cooled slowly
without its help, cracking and
creaking, though subtly, the metals
and alloys contracting yet again,
just as slow, and all
at once the oak trees
had shed their leaves while
the wrens formed a little
community at the bird feeder
and the blood made its
rounds through the body, going,
still going, but noisier now.

Hook, Line, Sinker

Catgut: odd line to fish
or write with, holding up
a birdfeeder, not bank, not
corner petstore. In the air
behind a living room: suspended
sunflower seeds, all strung out
on a line, the feeder
bouncing under and with them
in wind or reacting to
the force of Steller's jays
landing hard or taking off.
Chickadees. Nuthatches. Who can see
that small difference, or hear?
Occasional quail beneath peck at
spilled seed – what an echo
has out of nowhere made
its way into this. Nights,
mice. By day, rats, only
at night peaceable. The eye
and mind, neither given nor
accepting peace, follow every time
the distractions of some creature
ghosting toward the feeder, first
taken, then taking, feeding, fed.

Nest

Only you and the wasps asleep,
the sun all red, still straining
to free itself from its cloud-cocoon.

No idea why insects become
the measure for my thinking
when the scale of things even here
tilts toward the cosmic:

the deceptive smooth grey
of water blends into smooth grey
of sky where horizon should be.

For lack of it, I hang on to
what I can: table, chair, lesser line
of the wall, good stone,
though recently shaken.

The wasps and you sleep away
into the evening until earth, sky
and water better define themselves.

There's plenty of time to fly.

Apparition

The racket of too many crows, answered
by a single raven's cry, higher:
you try to draw some thing out of it.

As if the evening sky were a window
that kept opening to let sound through,
or a door slowly closing.

And if window, which of its sides
would you find yourself on?
Which side, if door?

Time certainly passes; the sky
seems rather to close than to open.
To the apparent lightness, the clouds,
a raven adds the shifting weight of its wing.

You almost believe you can live
with such uncertainty, not succumb
to the image of a raven swarmed by crows,
and all the words that calls forth,
and the silence after.

Interference

If waves of light can cancel one another,
colour overlapping with colour into black,
why not sound waves?

The ear chooses to pick and choose.
What it ignores remains like a small, too bright
light, like something in peripheral hearing.

In the foreground now, the sportscaster
lets his voice on the killer loudspeakers
expand into the middle ground, fore- and back.

Huge breakers still break on the shore.
The stonemason still hammers his stones
into their cubic perfections. Nameless birds
still cry out for their names and sometimes
other birds answer.

Now is it bird or gecko noise?

When the ear bends to the ground, the mind
might begin to imagine the roar of black ants
making short work of a grasshopper carcass.

Or in a moment of inattention,
hear the earth's plates grinding into and over
one another, so hard that the ear refuses
and the mind goes blank.

Quinta do Cerrado

I.

Bars on the window cut daylight
into exact squares.
The shuddering eucalyptus
renders it approximate.

Shadow-bats flutter on the carpet,
butterflies, only more short-lived,
synapses of light and dark.

We stare at them and feel no need
to say what needs to be said.

In time, we make connections
between wind and shadow,
sun and tree.

Sometimes, when we fail to talk
it creates a balance like that.

II.

Snakes, the tiny ones – how sensitive
to sound. Through the eucalyptus woods,
we stamp our feet.

No wind. Packs of dogs rouse
one neighbourhood and then
a closer one. We're not alone
out here, walking.

Grasshoppers? Crickets? How explain
the small difference?

By late afternoon, rats stop chirping
and appear on the vines, as if light
had finally abandoned them.

We clap our hands to frighten them off,
maybe applaud their audacity,
and so reduce it.

The snakes, too, rustle away
at the mere sound of us.

III.

No wind. The glass of our world
mists over, whatever shifts behind it
shifting more slowly.

Too much sun has brought with it
too little clarity: even the gecko
cannot catch its own shadow.

We argue again and fail to agree
on the cause. Again.

Mosquitoes, stupid with our blood,
drone into sudden electric light;
we flatten them without much thought
or effort against white walls

and fall silent – caught by the blood?

Beyond the glass, a couple dances,
given this air,
and not much else to do.

Teen at the Mirror

Narcissus by the pond again, again grows
weary of reflections. Tired of rumours
about his phantom sister, and not at all
curious about the spaces she could fill
in his life, he lets others pursue that hint
of pain or loss to its larger conclusion,
or better drop it once and for all. Everyone
in his small circle has paired up with someone;
all belabour the agonies and wonders
of love. Yes, he can imagine well. Enough.
Hunched over the water as usual, he looks
at his image like some poet at a loss
for words, dimwit searching the surface as though
it would all by itself break open, reveal
suddenly meaningful depths. His face floats there
in two dimensions, the brow knit and unknit,
as the boy becoming a man behind it tries
to find new ways not to think what he's thinking.

Night Fishing

I.

Two lights bob on what looks
like nothing and must be water,
or bounce on the nothing that
water is. They make for a poor
constellation, hardly enough
to let us navigate through the night
or our dream of the silent fish
in silence nibbling away at it.

We assume the fish in darkness
approach the light, the way
deer do, or the proverbial moths
(much larger here, so
their light-struggle comes fiercer)
and the fishermen, the hunters
take them easily. Easy for them.

But see no men, no hunters,
no fish, except in the dream.
If there's agony between anything
here, it's between light and dark
as it always is.

II.

As Pacheco said, only Spanish (so far
as he knew) makes the distinction
between fish and fish caught, between
fish and catch (*pez, pescado*)

and maybe it follows in some language
that fishing differs also from fishing,
differs not the way night and day do,
but more like waiting and receiving,
like bite and tug on the line, or tug
on the line and something at its end,
hauled in.

     Pto. Escondido

Space Walk

He backs into the large space that defines
his small part in it,
cosmonaut drifting away
from the mother ship, little umbilicus
trailing behind, broken or cut.

This baby – no one says it, only thinks
and thinks – is going nowhere.

For a time, all the known stars in the universe
offer up their light to him.
For a minute or two he feels
the universe spin around its centre
loosening in his skull: less
and less oxygen.

The circumference remains nowhere
as the centre expands: space
reclaims itself even as it washes away
any sense of him.

Time's up! Everything else
points elsewhere, to the suns
and moons and the holes into which
their light disappears,
his thoughts close behind, too fast now
to make an order of them,
their acceleration,
their collapse.

Three Attitudes

I.

How singular, each
living in the first person,
she for herself,
he for him,

eyes open, drawing
no distinctions between
sight and vision.

What truths, then,
in mere grass,
her green, his green,
those separate expanses.

What lies at night,
his blue and her blue
drawn from one ocean

on which she finds boats
and ships that come in.

He only sees them go.

II.

Whatever she has just composed
makes for the edge, juts
toward the frame and threatens
to continue into his space,

brush still in her hand,
the heavy paint on it.

Imitation table, sudden cat,
cartoonish,

and two chairs on which to sit
or lean back to admire the work,
composed once more,
stroking, stroking,
testing the distance

until everything purrs.

III.

They keep returning
to the simple:

candlewax, daydream, sunlight,

and give themselves up
to what's simpler still:

wax, light.

They take daily impressions
with them into night,
retinal sun, skin tingling
into spasm and sleep,

and press back,
half accepting, half resisting
whatever might attach itself

to render them complex again.

Deadhead

i.

All praise to the teredo, its work
long finished and ongoing,
a likeness for anything you want.

Not just the head – the whole body
feels the effect, even the heart.

The teredo, alone true to its purpose,
does not let go, as that person did
who felled this tree only to lose it.

Praise too: barnacles, mussels, hands
of a man drowning or one only swimming,
each searching here and there for a hold.

II.

The head: borne sometimes like a child
or bony old man on the shoulders,
suffered like a son or a father,
uncle, more distant relative, his advice
too much given and just as much
not taken.

The head, then, like an old man
out of his head and talking, talking,
his words never catching up
to their long-forgotten intention.

And just when it's become too old
or too wise to offer further resistance
the body remembers
the heart's equal burden.

III.

As if all the elements endured
the same weight: water above,
water below, everything adrift
without marker or light.

A constant drone, as of ships, liquid.
Boats also, with lesser destinations,
smaller schedules.

And if one of them sinks, what
does it serve?

Adrift, therefore aimless, but
it's only wood, a deadhead.

Of consciousness: no question.
Of questions: none.

Just wood in the dependable water,
cool, saline, like nearly everything
in this hypothesis.

The salt, like everything
you touch, every wound
you welcome,
rubbing it in.

IV.

Quick to fog up, slow to clear:
the head nods,
nods no matter what.

Light conditions the air
the head takes in.

It agrees to all the conditions.

And then a drop of rain, the tap
tap on the skull that sets it
going again:

a mouth imagined inside
whispers into an imagined ear,
its mouth whispering too
and so on until the real mouth
cries *Rain!* and the heart
begins to dissolve in it.

Tribute

A night the way Mandelstam might have composed it:
overpowering and with bells in bell towers:

all the names of God should be fluttering within,
along with bats that cast no shadow – the world, then,

though absence, turns to presence, canvas on which paint
begins to suggest itself, vacuum for the self,

constantly *poor* thing, to try to fill.   An ocean
that the silence suggests becomes material,

and with breasts, no less!   The impoverished self suckles,
sucks like an infant or bivalve – more generous

trope that renders ego, not all the world, oyster,
to allow pearls to form within the nightly flesh.

What here attaches itself to what?   Mandelstam
writes nothing of the necessary abrasions

which begin a process that makes dawn come early,
blue-grey at first, or grey or blue alone, rendering

the complex possibilities of metaphor simpler:
a point of view,   a horizon,   a sky.

Penelope, Still Waiting

Closer to home the death bells had not begun tolling.

Even the brightest stars required no window to contain them,
nor sun and moon a door.

No gecko found shelter behind a lantern mounted high
on a whitewashed wall along which the pissing dogs
fell more readily into their species, and she knew them
for their bark and their bite.

She listened to the speeches all around and allowed
her ear to select its own favourite passages.

The carefully chosen language avoided the invisible spines,
if not the blossom, of the cactus, if only because
its Latinate name had escaped her memory again.

If blood lines still held the ancient families together,
she could not trace them.

Certain tricks of a kinder light she ignored,
as she did the trickster the light left only half revealed.

High above, the vapours of transatlantic jets trailed
as always, gathering around particles of dust
while electrons spun according to the familiar models,
though outdated, that she still half-remembered.

Snow-capped mountains in the distance built up
their positive – or was it negative – charge
of which thick clouds at last released them.

Closer, down below, aphids forced her eye
round a leaf's convolutions.

Though she would never say so, she preferred
to remain here, letting her eye take less ambitious flight,
out over the blue, through waves of nothing but light
pounding toward impossible cliffs
and breaking down their resistance:

perpetually new world.

She wandered along the top of the cliffs or below
and gave them no further thought.

Snake pits apparent there were of kelp merely
and had only imagined victims or patients
and only when she cared to imagine.

Granite for the new bell tower had all been imported,
like the European starling, which she despised
for its pitiful song, even if sung
with its simplest of black voices.

The diesel of the one yacht coming or going
on the horizon appeared to be the single engine
that kept her whole planet turning.

Night Window

I.

Of all the stars framed in it,
just one shoots away,
leaving an absence
you dream toward,
slowly.

Of all dreams,
this one proves best.

II.

Black of what seems air held
in place by black of what seems
wrought iron. The welded joint
still glows with cosmic heat
you remember:

long day far off.

Sparks here do not fly, but hang,
hanging on to their fire,
colours shifting through the full
prismatic scale.

And all at once, a star shoots
out of the frame, *its* weld weakened
by fitful sleep.

When the star falls back
into place again, your fitful waking
will keep it there.

III.

Half moon floating slowly in it,
right to left, right to left,
ever closer to the heart,

while the mind drifts left
to right, resisting.

Where do the missing halves go?

Stars, of course, hang on
when the moon's all gone.

Into their silence, the small
sound of your breathing,
as the part of you I only guess
goes flying after them.

Iron blackens around the last of the day,
its rust eating away what light remains.

Ornate curves ease some of the pain
of loss, the glass behind stalling the cold,
toward morning more and more bitter.

No way around Lao Tzu's formulation:
the useful part of the wall lies
in what's not there.
The useful part of the night.
The useful part of the day.

In the near-perfect black of night,
a near-perfect starlight prevails.

By the time the earth has completed
another rotation, the restored light
will help balance your mood
as you ponder the loss, and the gain.

V.

The constellations break apart within,
snatches of them wrested away from the whole
that, so near the equator, makes no sense
to us. North has become an idea no Big Dipper
we can find leads us back to. The Great Bear
has no nocturnal cave to dwell in down here.

Groote Beer: name of the ship, Holland-
America Line, that sailed from Rotterdam
to Quebec City in 1952 – I know where
this memory comes from. Where does it lead?

The stars shift left to right in the window.
The earth still spins. Each time the head rises
from the pillow – an intruder? Only a gecko clicking? –
a new star loosens from the night and flashes
like a firefly or errant satellite in the mind's directions.

Flashes and burns. Then loosens from the mind
and fixes itself to where the larger design
would have it, while the lesser fever, which wants it
not still, goes up in its own light and away from it.

Acknowledgements

Thanks to the editors and staff of the following periodicals in which poems in this book, or earlier versions of them, first appeared: *Arc*, *Canadian Fiction Magazine*, *Canadian Literature*, *Descant*, *Event*, *The Fiddlehead*, *Grain*, *The Literary Review* (USA), *The Malahat Review*, *The Nashwaak Review*, *Prism international*, and *Southern Review* (Australia), and to the Hawthorn Society for producing *Door Slowly Closing*, a chapbook in which "Apparition," "Dream of the State of the World," and "Tropical Snowman" first appeared.

Thanks to Don Mowatt for so ably incorporating parts of "Some People Going Somewhere" into a sequence, "Postcards from Lisbon," broadcast on the CBC's *On the Arts*.

The final shape of this work owes much to John Donlan's generous reading and gentle nudging, for which I thank him especially.

Biography:

Derk Wynand was born in Bad Suderode, Germany in 1944 and has lived in Canada since 1952. The author of several works of poetry, fiction, and translation, and a former editor of *The Malahat Review*, he teaches in the Department of Writing at the University of Victoria. Brick Books published Wynand's *Closer to Home* in 1997.